LEGACY BUILDERS

ADRIANA LUNA CARLOS
Editor-In-Chief, Designer
and Co-Founder

HANNA OLIVAS
Managing Editor &
Co-Founder

ADVERTISING OPPORTUNITIES

Info@SheRisesStudios.com

LEGACY WOMAN
JANUARY 2026

SHE RISES
S T U D I O S

CONTACT US

editorial@sherisesstudios.com

WWW.SHERISESSTUDIOS.COM

LETTER FROM THE EDITORS

Dear Reader,

Legacy is not built in comfort.

It is built in the moments that test us, shape us, and ask us who we are willing to become.

The inaugural January 2026 issue of Legacy Builders Magazine, Where Purpose Becomes Permanent, is devoted to leaders who understand that legacy is not accidental. It is intentional. It is forged through hardship, clarified through healing, and sustained through courage and integrity. This issue honors those who do not simply survive life's disruptions, but transform them into foundations for lasting impact.

Our cover feature, Debi Lynn, embodies this truth with extraordinary clarity. A Business Resilience Strategist and Certified Grief Educator, Debi brings a voice that is both powerful and deeply human. Her leadership was not born from theory alone, but from profound loss, burnout, and identity upheaval. Rather than allowing pain to silence her, Debi chose to listen to it, learn from it, and build something meaningful in its wake.

Debi teaches that women are not broken when life knocks them down, they are buried. And buried things, when nurtured, still grow. Her work reframes grief, burnout, and disruption not as endpoints, but as data, as teachers, and as catalysts for rebuilding power on one's own terms. Through her guidance, resilience becomes more than survival; it becomes strategy, clarity, and sustainable leadership.

This edition of Legacy Builders Magazine celebrates leaders who build with intention, who honor both heart and structure, and who understand that emotional resilience is not a soft skill, it is the bedrock of longevity. Across these pages, you will encounter stories of women who chose honesty over hiding, healing over hustle, and purpose over performance.

Legacy is not measured only by what we create.

It is measured by what we heal, who we uplift, and what we leave standing long after we are gone.

Welcome to Legacy Builders Magazine.
This is where purpose becomes permanent.

Adriana Luna Carlos & Hanna Olivas
Editors of Legacy Builders Magazine

Become a Managing Partner

she wins
WOMEN'S NETWORK

Join a global Movement of Visionary Women
50+ Chapters. Transformative Community. Unlimited Growth.

WHAT'S INCLUDED

- 40% commission on memberships + event bonuses
- Leadership training, toolkits & ongoing support
- VIP access to retreats, masterminds & more

Join for just

www.shewinswomensnetwork.com

Application Fee (paid only after acceptance)

DEBI LYNN

FROM BURIED TO BECOMING— REDEFINING POWER, LEADERSHIP, AND RESILIENCE THROUGH GRIEF

By **She Rises Studios Editorial Team**

Heart-Led AWAKENING

Debi Lynn's work is grounded in a belief that challenges one of the most persistent narratives placed on women in pain. Women, she teaches, are not broken. They are buried. And buried things, when given the right conditions, still grow. This philosophy was not born from theory or training alone. It emerged from the most devastating season of her life, when everything she knew collapsed at once and forced her to reimagine not only who she was, but how leadership, purpose, and success could be defined.

That moment came when Debi lost her son, Robert. With that loss, she also lost the version of herself she believed she was supposed to be. Soon after, her job disappeared. Her business followed. The sense of safety and identity she had carefully built unraveled. From the outside, she tried to remain strong and keep moving forward. Inside, she felt buried under layers of grief, fear, and shame. Then, in a quiet moment alone, a realization surfaced that would change the trajectory of her life and work. She was not broken. She was planted. The pain was not there to end her, but to grow something new.

That realization shifted the questions she asked herself. Instead of wondering what was wrong with her, Debi began asking what the pain was teaching her. In that space, she discovered that power is not loud, purpose is not rushed, and profit does not come from pushing through pain but from healing it first. When she chose to heal, her voice returned. When her voice returned, her work was born. And when she began leading from her heart, everything changed.

Grief reshaped Debi's understanding of leadership at its core.

Losing her son stripped away any illusion that leaders must appear unshakable or untouched by pain. She learned that real leadership is not about never falling, but about being willing to feel, heal, and still show up with honesty. Grief removed the need to look strong and replaced it with the courage to be real. Through her own experience and through walking alongside other women, she saw how pain can soften the heart while sharpening wisdom. It cultivates compassion, patience, and a quiet strength that does not need volume to be powerful.

Because of this, Debi's definition of legacy is deeply human. She is not driven by titles, numbers, or recognition. Her vision is to leave behind spaces where women feel safe telling the truth about their pain without shame. She wants leadership to look like empathy, presence, and permission to be whole. In the resilience space, her legacy is measured by whether women feel seen, supported, and strong enough to rise again after life knocks them down.

This philosophy also shapes how Debi approaches business. After her world fell apart, she initially tried to lead the same way she always had. The result was exhaustion, numbness, and diminishing focus. Her work suffered. Her confidence faded. It became clear that pushing harder was not strength. It was self-betrayal. When she finally slowed down and faced what she was feeling, clarity returned. Her decisions improved. Her energy came back. That was when she understood that emotional resilience is not a soft skill. It is a strategic advantage.

Debi learned that when a woman can regulate her emotions, she can lead under pressure, make clean decisions, and build with intention. Emotional resilience creates trust, prevents burnout, and allows businesses to be sustainable instead of fragile. Once she stopped separating feelings from strategy, her business became calmer, stronger, and more aligned. Today, she teaches resilience not as an optional add-on, but as the foundation everything else stands on.

With experience spanning emotional wellness, supply chain management, and government contracting, Debi bridges the gap between operational efficiency and heart-centered leadership in a way few can. She helps leaders understand that people are the system. In high-stakes environments, she saw firsthand that efficiency breaks down when emotions are ignored. Missed deadlines, poor decisions, and high turnover often signal burnout rather than incompetence. When leaders address emotional load with the same care they give budgets and timelines, operations run cleaner and faster.

Inside the organizations she supports, structure and empathy coexist. Clear expectations, strong processes, and accountability remain, but they are led with presence and care. When people feel seen and supported, they show up sharper, more focused, and more loyal. The results are measurable: productivity rises, retention improves, and decision-making strengthens. Operational excellence sustains the system. Heart-centered leadership empowers the people who run it.

Debi often says she did not just survive pain, she built a business on it. In the earliest days, she made a simple but powerful choice. She stopped hiding her pain and started learning from it. She paid attention to what helped her through the hardest days and what made things worse. She focused on regulating her nervous system before trying to fix anything else. That shift reframed her experience from falling apart to being rebuilt. Pain became data, not a dead end.

From there, she created repeatable, real structures around healing, clarity, and action. Step by step, she rebuilt energy, confidence, and focus. As her strength returned, so did her ability to lead and earn. The framework she now teaches was born not from theory, but from lived experience. What once knocked her down became the foundation that helps other women rise, rebuild, and create lasting success.

In a world that pressures leaders to appear unshakable, Debi offers a different path. She teaches powerhouse women that being unshakable does not mean being untouched. Strength comes from knowing how to steady yourself when things shake. Her work begins with grounding, breathing, and naming what is real. By creating emotional safety inside first, women show up calmer, clearer, and more confident, even in crisis. Strength, she teaches, is presence, not perfection. Clarity, not control.

Debi is also one of the few voices speaking openly about grief in the workplace. Unprocessed grief, she explains, shows up in burnout, brain fog, disengagement, missed deadlines, and high turnover. It is not limited to death, but includes identity loss, role changes, health issues, and sudden life disruptions. When organizations suppress grief, it leaks into performance and culture. When they acknowledge it, safety replaces silence. Energy once spent hiding pain is reclaimed, and resilience becomes real, sustainable, and deeply human.

Even the lighter, unexpected parts of Debi's story matter. Winning donkey basketball and mastering Hollywood-worthy pin curls are reminders that identity is bigger than loss. Humor and play help women remember who they were before survival mode took over. Laughter creates space to breathe again. Bold moments rebuild confidence. Joy, she teaches, is not betrayal of grief. It is a pathway back to self.

Looking back, the most transformational habit shaping Debi's legacy is choosing honesty over hiding. Each day, she checks in with herself before leading anyone else. This practice keeps her grounded, aligned, and real. It allows her to lead from integrity rather than image. That honesty gives other women permission to do the same.

Ultimately, Debi Lynn hopes her work teaches the next generation of women leaders that they do not have to abandon themselves to succeed. Feeling deeply is not a weakness. It is wisdom. If her work helps even one woman stop shaming herself for pain and start using it as fuel for clarity, courage, and impact, then the legacy lives on. Women are not broken. They are becoming.

Connect With Debi

www.facebook.com/debitx
www.linkedin.com/in/debi-lynn-tv-host-producer-5b897b208
www.instagram.com/debi.lynntexas
www.youtube.com/@FIGfriendsingrief
www.friendsingrief.com
www.debilyntx.com
www.debilynnfl.com
www.heartledawakening.com

BRUNCH & BOSS UP™

Brunch & Boss Up™ is not your average talk show—it's a bold, live YouTube experience filmed at high-energy brunch events across the U.S. Designed for the modern entrepreneur, each episode brings together a rotating cast of inspiring business owners, thought leaders, and creatives for real, unfiltered conversations in front of a live audience.

Expect candid stories, fun games, and breakthrough moments—served with mimosas, good food, and great company.

A LIVE BRUNCH SHOW ABOUT REAL ENTREPRENEURS, REAL STORIES, AND BOSS-LEVEL ENERGY

WHERE ELSE CAN YOU SIP MIMOSAS, SHARE STORIES, AND SPARK BREAKTHROUGHS OVER BRUNCH?

Brunch & Boss Up™ is a bold new live YouTube show filmed at high-energy brunch events across the U.S.— where entrepreneurs, creatives, and change-makers come together to eat, laugh, connect, and rise.

Hosted by Hanna Olivas and Adriana Luna Carlos, founders of She Rises Studios and FENIX TV, the show is a natural extension of their mission to empower women globally through storytelling, media, and community. Together, they create spaces where women feel seen, heard, and inspired to lead boldly.

Each episode is filmed in front of a live audience and features a rotating lineup of powerhouse guests who bring their stories, insights, and unfiltered truths to the table. It's where personality meets purpose, and where mimosas meet the mic.

From hilarious games and real conversations to unexpected breakthroughs, Brunch & Boss Up™ is equal parts fun, fierce, and uplifting.

Think Red Table Talk meets UpDating—with a shot of a mimosa and a whole lot of hustle.

Hosted by dynamic duo Hanna Olivas and Adriana Luna Carlos, the show brings their signature energy and heart to every city it touches. Each event is designed to celebrate connection, elevate voices, and create space for meaningful growth and collaboration.

Want to be part of the cast?

We're looking for 4–6 bold, dynamic entrepreneurs in each city to join the show.

As a featured cast member, you'll be:

- On stage, live with our hosts
- Part of the games, challenges, and conversations
- Featured on YouTube and across our social media
- Celebrated for your energy, personality, and story— not just your business

Brunch & Boss Up™ is coming to cities near you.

DAVID GREEN

BUILDING LEGACY THROUGH FAITH, BUSINESS, AND PHILANTHROPY

By **She Rises Studios Editorial Team**

In the January 2026 issue of *Legacy Builders Magazine*, themed *Built to Last: The Power of Intentional Legacy*, David Green exemplifies how business success, guided by purpose and faith, can create a lasting impact on communities and culture. Based in Oklahoma City, OK, Green is the co-founder of Hobby Lobby, a company that has grown into one of America's most recognized retail brands. Beyond corporate achievement, his leadership is defined by a commitment to philanthropy, education, and the preservation of cultural and religious heritage, demonstrating that legacy is built through intentional action and service.

Green's journey began with a vision to create a business that not only delivers quality products but also reflects values-driven leadership. Under his guidance, Hobby Lobby has become synonymous with integrity, strategic growth, and a commitment to employee development. Green believes that a successful business serves a higher purpose, and he has consistently applied this principle by integrating faith-based initiatives into corporate decision-making. For him, business and legacy are inseparable—profit is a means to empower communities and enact positive change.

Philanthropy is central to Green's legacy-building philosophy. Through generous contributions to education, arts, and faith-based programs, he invests in the growth and development of others, ensuring that his success extends far beyond the boardroom. Green's philanthropic efforts focus on both immediate impact and long-term cultural preservation, reflecting a vision of legacy that transcends individual achievement. By championing initiatives that provide resources, opportunities, and guidance, he exemplifies how leaders can multiply their influence through intentional giving.

Education plays a pivotal role in Green's approach to mentorship and legacy. He emphasizes the importance of equipping future generations with both practical skills and moral grounding. From supporting educational programs to funding initiatives that nurture leadership and creativity, Green's contributions demonstrate a commitment to preparing others for sustainable success. This aligns perfectly with the *Legacy Builders Magazine* theme, *Built to Last: The Power of Intentional Legacy*, which highlights how thoughtful guidance and strategic support can transform individual accomplishments into enduring societal impact.

Green also underscores the importance of values-driven leadership. His approach integrates faith, ethics, and operational excellence, proving that principled leadership can coexist with commercial growth. By fostering a corporate culture that prioritizes integrity, accountability, and social responsibility, Green has built a company that not only thrives economically but also serves as a model for how purpose and profit can align. This blend of strategic thinking and moral vision exemplifies the essence of building a lasting legacy.

As 2026 begins, David Green continues to inspire leaders to view success as a platform for service. His life's work demonstrates that legacy is not simply what one achieves personally—

it is the enduring impact created through mentorship, philanthropy, and purposeful leadership. By championing education, preserving culture, and uplifting communities, Green ensures that his influence extends well beyond the marketplace, creating systems, opportunities, and guidance for generations to come.

David Green's career is a reminder that intentional legacy combines vision, values, and action. Through faith-driven leadership, strategic business acumen, and a deep commitment to philanthropy, he transforms personal success into collective growth. In doing so, Green embodies the core principle of *Legacy Builders Magazine*: that true legacy is designed, nurtured, and sustained when leaders actively lift others as they build their own paths.

www.sherisesstudios.com

© SUE OGROCKI

JANICE BRYANT HOWROYD

BUILDING A LEGACY THAT LASTS

By **She Rises Studios Editorial Team**

In the January 2026 edition of *Legacy Builders Magazine*, themed *Built to Last: The Power of Intentional Legacy*, Janice Bryant Howroyd stands as a quintessential example of how vision, determination, and mentorship converge to create enduring impact. As the founder of ActOne Group and the first Black woman to build a billion-dollar staffing company, Howroyd's career is a testament to the power of purpose-driven leadership, strategic growth, and lifting others along the way.

Janice Bryant Howroyd's journey began with a simple but transformative vision: to create opportunities for people and businesses alike. From humble beginnings, she launched ActOne Group with the goal of connecting talent to opportunity, particularly in underserved communities. Over the years, the company grew into a global enterprise with a diverse portfolio of staffing, workforce solutions, and consulting services. Her success, however, is measured not only by revenue or scale but by the countless lives she has positively impacted through employment, mentorship, and leadership development programs.

Mentorship lies at the core of Howroyd's leadership philosophy. She actively invests time, resources, and guidance into emerging leaders, particularly women and people of color seeking to navigate complex professional landscapes. Howroyd believes that knowledge and opportunity should be intentionally transferred, creating a multiplier effect that strengthens communities, industries, and future generations. By mentoring others, she ensures that her legacy extends beyond the tangible success of ActOne Group, embedding influence into the lives and careers of those she guides.

Beyond mentorship, Howroyd's leadership is defined by a deliberate approach to workforce development. She emphasizes skills-building, professional growth, and economic empowerment as pillars of lasting impact. Through innovative programs, partnerships, and training initiatives, she equips employees and business leaders with the tools needed to thrive in dynamic markets. Her approach demonstrates that legacy is not an abstract concept—it is built through consistent action, strategic planning, and investments in people that compound over time.

Howroyd also embodies the principles of intentional legacy through her advocacy and thought leadership. She regularly speaks on issues of entrepreneurship, diversity, and inclusion, offering insights that challenge the status quo and inspire systemic change. Her public presence amplifies the importance of equity in business, encouraging organizations and leaders to prioritize long-term impact alongside immediate success. By connecting her personal story to broader lessons in leadership, she ensures that her experiences serve as a blueprint for others aspiring to create meaningful change.

In addition to building a thriving global enterprise, Howroyd's influence extends into philanthropic and civic initiatives. She leverages her platform to support causes that enhance education, workforce readiness, and economic equity. These efforts align seamlessly with the magazine's theme, reinforcing the idea that a purposeful legacy combines personal achievement with a commitment to uplift others.

As we reflect on the start of 2026, Janice Bryant Howroyd exemplifies how intentional leadership

© STARTUP GUIDE

can transform ambition into lasting significance. Her story proves that true legacy is not accidental; it is designed through vision, integrity, and deliberate mentorship. Every connection she fosters, every opportunity she creates, and every life she touches contributes to an enduring influence that transcends her own accomplishments.

Janice Bryant Howroyd's career is a blueprint for building a legacy that lasts. By centering mentorship, workforce development, and generational economic impact, she demonstrates that real success is measured not only in milestones achieved but in the people empowered along the way. Her life's work embodies the essence of *Built to Last*, reminding us all that when leadership is intentional, its impact echoes across generations.

JOIN THE SHE RISES STUDIOS COMMUNITY

SCAN TO JOIN

Daily motivation, expert insights, and sisterhood support come together in one empowering space. Connect, empower, and thrive—whether you're an entrepreneur, professional, or simply seeking inspiration, this is your place to grow!

You don't have to do it alone—let's rise together!

THE SHE RISES STUDIOS
PODCAST

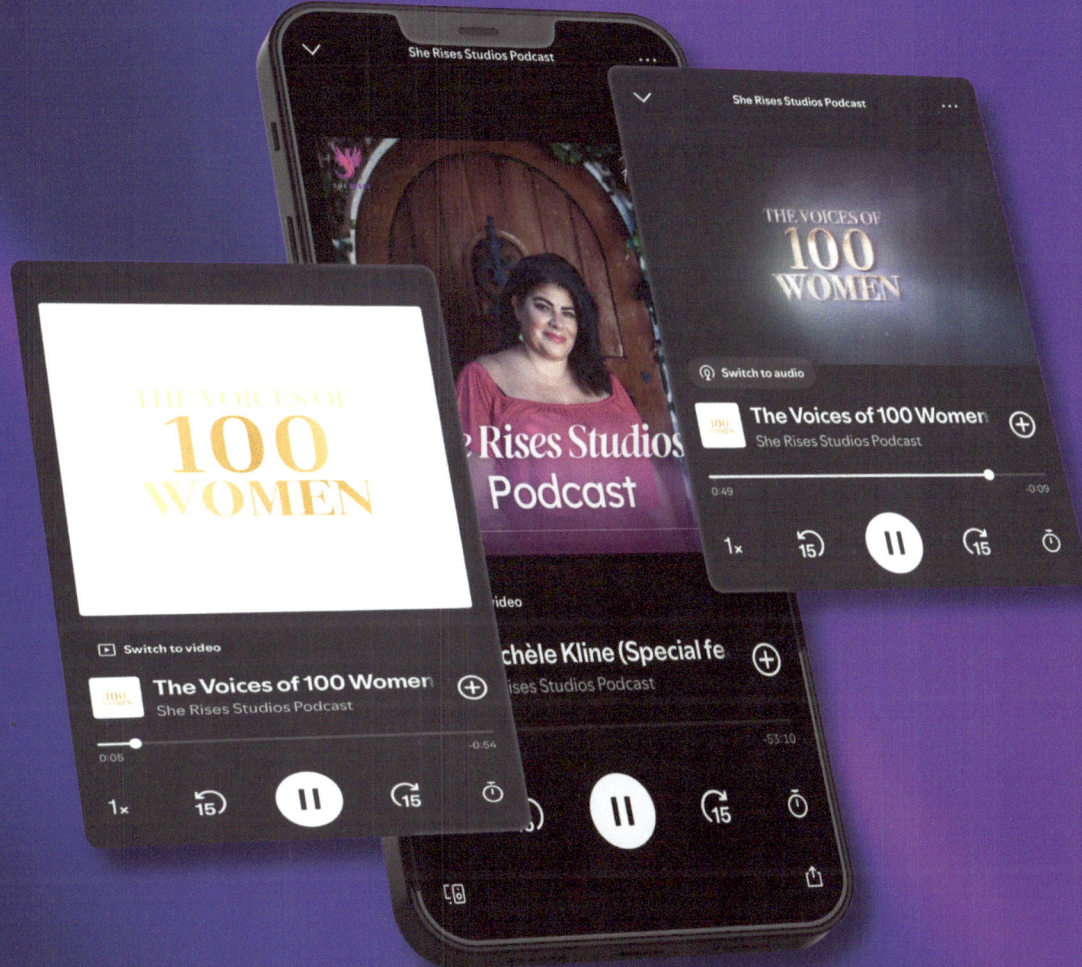

Each episode of the She Rises Studios Podcast delivers real stories, expert insights, and actionable strategies to help you step into your power and create the life you desire. This isn't just a podcast—it's your roadmap to confidence, success, and purpose.

Through powerful interviews with trailblazing entrepreneurs, thought leaders, and inspiring women, we dive deep into conversations that spark growth, fuel ambition, and ignite your potential. If you're ready to rise higher and live boldly, you're in the right place.

SUBSCRIBE NOW AND START YOUR JOURNEY TO EMPOWERMENT!

JIM STEGALL

ALIGNING LEADERSHIP WITH LASTING IMPACT

By **She Rises Studios Editorial Team**

© UCSB SUMMER SESSIONS

In the January 2026 edition of *Legacy Builders Magazine*, themed *Built to Last: The Power of Intentional Legacy*, Jim Stegall exemplifies how visionary leadership and purposeful strategy can create a legacy that transcends business success. Based in Nashville, TN, Stegall has dedicated his career to helping entrepreneurs and leaders align profit with long-term purpose, ensuring that their work not only drives financial results but also meaningful community impact.

Stegall's approach to leadership is both strategic and heart-centered. He believes that businesses thrive when they operate with intention—when goals are aligned with values and success is measured not just in revenue but in the positive influence they create.

Through his work as a leadership strategist and philanthropy advocate, Stegall partners with entrepreneurs to develop frameworks that integrate operational efficiency, sustainable growth, and social responsibility. His methodology emphasizes that true legacy is built when leaders intentionally design systems that uplift others while achieving their business vision.

Mentorship is at the core of Stegall's philosophy. He actively guides emerging entrepreneurs and seasoned leaders alike, helping them navigate complex decisions while staying grounded in their purpose. Stegall teaches that mentorship is a force multiplier: by investing in the growth and development of others,

leaders not only strengthen their organizations but also leave a lasting imprint on their communities. His influence has helped countless founders transform their ideas into thriving enterprises that balance profitability with positive social impact.

Stegall's work also highlights the importance of strategic philanthropy as a pillar of enduring legacy. He encourages leaders to integrate giving into their organizational models, whether through formal foundations, corporate social responsibility initiatives, or community partnerships. By aligning philanthropic efforts with company missions, Stegall demonstrates how leaders can create systemic change, turning businesses into vehicles for long-term societal benefit.

Beyond consulting and mentorship, Stegall serves as a thought leader, sharing insights on leadership, purpose-driven entrepreneurship, and the intersection of business and community impact. His guidance emphasizes the alignment of personal and organizational values, showing that when profit and purpose coexist, leaders can achieve sustainable success while positively influencing others.

In his view, a lasting legacy is crafted through deliberate action, intentional mentorship, and a commitment to improving both people's lives and the broader ecosystem in which a business operates.

As 2026 begins, Jim Stegall's work serves as a blueprint for leaders who aspire to build enterprises and careers that endure. His focus on mentorship, purpose-driven strategy, and philanthropy reflects the magazine's theme, *Built to Last: The Power of Intentional Legacy*, reminding readers that legacy is not an automatic byproduct of success—it is designed through vision, values, and meaningful action.

Jim Stegall exemplifies how leadership can be both bold and benevolent. By helping entrepreneurs align profit with purpose and embedding philanthropy into business practices, he proves that sustainable success is possible when leaders prioritize people, community, and long-term impact. His career is a testament to the power of intentionality, mentorship, and service, offering a roadmap for anyone seeking to leave a legacy that truly matters.

www.sherisesstudios.com

LORI GREINER

MENTORSHIP AND INNOVATION FOR LASTING BUSINESS LEGACY

By **She Rises Studios Editorial Team**

In the January 2026 issue of *Legacy Builders Magazine*, themed *Built to Last: The Power of Intentional Legacy*, Lori Greiner stands out as a shining example of how mentorship, innovation, and strategic guidance can transform entrepreneurial dreams into enduring success. Based in Chicago, IL, Greiner has spent decades cultivating her reputation as a powerhouse inventor, investor, and mentor, helping countless entrepreneurs turn ideas into thriving businesses while emphasizing the importance of building legacies that last.

Greiner, often referred to as the *"Queen of QVC,"* is known for her keen eye for innovative products and her ability to scale them into household names. But beyond her commercial achievements, it is her dedication to empowering others that defines her leadership. Through mentorship and education, she equips entrepreneurs with the skills, confidence, and insight they need to navigate the complexities of launching and sustaining a business. For Greiner, success is not measured solely in profits, but in the impact and opportunities created for the next generation of innovators.

At the heart of Greiner's approach is mentorship as a multiplier of success. She actively guides emerging entrepreneurs through product development, branding, and business strategy, offering practical wisdom drawn from her own experiences. Her mentorship style balances encouragement with accountability, instilling both the creative courage and disciplined execution that are essential for lasting business impact. By investing in others, Greiner amplifies her influence and ensures that knowledge and opportunity are passed forward, creating a ripple effect that extends far beyond individual ventures.

Education is another cornerstone of Greiner's legacy-building philosophy. She frequently shares insights on entrepreneurship, product innovation, and market strategy through publishing, speaking engagements, and media appearances. Her guidance provides entrepreneurs with the tools they need to make informed decisions, refine their strategies, and scale sustainably. By focusing on knowledge transfer, Greiner ensures that her mentorship is not transactional but transformative, helping founders not only succeed in the short term but build businesses capable of long-term growth and resilience.

Greiner's career also underscores the importance of blending creativity with operational savvy. As an inventor and investor, she demonstrates that innovation is most powerful when paired with strategic execution and market understanding. Her investments are not only financial—they are extensions of her mission to elevate entrepreneurial talent, creating businesses that can thrive independently while maintaining their founders' vision and values.

As 2026 unfolds, Lori Greiner exemplifies how leaders can intentionally craft legacy through mentorship, education, and hands-on guidance. Her work reflects the *Legacy Builders Magazine* theme, *Built to Last: The Power of Intentional Legacy*, showing that enduring influence is built not only through personal achievement but through empowering others to rise, innovate, and lead.

Greiner's model proves that legacy is designed, nurtured, and multiplied when leaders commit to lifting others as they ascend.

Lori Greiner's journey reminds us that success is most meaningful when shared. By mentoring entrepreneurs, educating future leaders, and championing innovation, she transforms individual achievements into collective growth. Her career is a testament to the power of intentional leadership, proving that true legacy is not merely what you create for yourself—but what you leave in the hands, minds, and futures of others.

www.sherisesstudios.com

© IMDB

SHE RISES
S T U D I O S

$\mathcal{U}$NLEASH YOUR STORY
BECOME A PUBLISHED AUTHOR!

Have you ever dreamed of sharing your wisdom, experience, or passion with the world? **Now is your time!**

Publishing a book isn't just about writing—it's about **establishing your authority, inspiring others, and creating a lasting legac**y. Plus, with the **$138.5 billion book industry** booming, there's never been a better moment to step into the spotlight.

At **SRS Publishing**, we don't just publish books—we **elevate voices, empower authors, and create change-makers**. Our mission is to help women break barriers, amplify their stories, and thrive in the publishing world. Whether you're an entrepreneur, thought leader, or storyteller at heart, **we're here to guide you every step of the way.**

JOIN THE FASTEST-GROWING PUBLISHING HOUSE FOR WOMEN IN THE USA.

READY TO TURN YOUR DREAM INTO REALITY?

 www.SheRisesStudios.com | contact@sherisesstudios.com

FENIX TV
YOUR PLATFORM, YOUR VOICE, YOUR POWER!

STEP INTO THE SPOTLIGHT AS A HOST ON FENIX TV!

Are you ready to amplify your message, inspire others, and be part of a groundbreaking network dedicated to empowering women worldwide? FENIX TV is your platform to shine as a host, share your expertise, and connect with a global audience.

WHY HOST ON FENIX TV?

- Reach a worldwide audience passionate about empowerment
- Showcase your voice, brand, and expertise
- Join a community of inspiring leaders and changemakers
- Be part of a network that uplifts and celebrates women

Whether you dream of leading a talk show, sharing powerful stories, or educating and inspiring others—FENIX TV is where your voice matters!

SECURE YOUR SPOT TODAY!

 Contact us now at
info@fenixtv.app

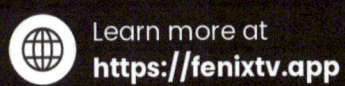 Learn more at
https://fenixtv.app

TINA SHARKEY

MENTORING THE NEXT WAVE OF PURPOSE-DRIVEN ENTREPRENEURS

By **She Rises Studios Editorial Team**

In the January 2026 issue of *Sheconomy™ Magazine*, themed *The Power of Transfer: Building the Next Economy*, Tina Sharkey embodies the essence of mentorship, innovation, and purposeful entrepreneurship. Based in New York, NY, Sharkey has built a reputation as a visionary tech entrepreneur and advisor, recognized for creating sustainable companies that balance growth, impact, and values. Beyond her own ventures, she dedicates herself to mentoring the next generation of founders, proving that leadership is as much about transferring knowledge and opportunity as it is about personal achievement.

Sharkey's entrepreneurial journey is defined by her ability to spot gaps in markets and create solutions that endure. She has co-founded and scaled multiple companies, emphasizing sustainable growth, customer-centric design, and mission-driven business models. Yet what truly sets Sharkey apart is her commitment to mentorship. She invests time, insight, and guidance in emerging founders, particularly women and underrepresented entrepreneurs, ensuring that innovation is accompanied by support, strategy, and resilience.

Mentorship, for Sharkey, is more than advice—it's a deliberate transfer of wisdom and networks. She models how experienced leaders can accelerate the growth of others by sharing lessons learned, opening doors, and cultivating confidence. Through her work, aspiring entrepreneurs gain access to strategies, frameworks, and mindsets that are often invisible until taught by someone who has navigated the complexities of scaling a business. Sharkey's mentorship philosophy aligns seamlessly with *Sheconomy™*'s January theme, which highlights how economic empowerment and leadership transfer are the cornerstones of the next-generation economy.

Sharkey also exemplifies sustainable entrepreneurship. Her ventures are not solely focused on short-term gains but are designed to create lasting impact in both markets and communities. By embedding sustainability, social responsibility, and ethical leadership into the core of her companies, she demonstrates how purpose-driven business can thrive while benefiting employees, customers, and society at large. This approach reflects the magazine's emphasis on collective growth as the currency of success and showcases how intentional leadership can scale far beyond individual achievement.

In addition to building sustainable companies, Sharkey is a sought-after advisor and thought leader in the tech and startup ecosystem. She shares her expertise on corporate boards, at industry conferences, and through mentorship programs, creating opportunities for founders to learn from her experience. Her influence extends beyond the companies she builds; it shapes the broader entrepreneurial ecosystem by inspiring a culture of guidance, collaboration, and shared success.

As the new year begins, Sharkey's work underscores the principle that true legacy is created when leaders actively lift others while building their own enterprises. By mentoring emerging founders, promoting sustainable business practices, and championing inclusive growth, she ensures that the next wave of entrepreneurs is prepared not only to succeed but to lead with integrity and impact.

Tina Sharkey's career is a masterclass in the power of leadership transfer. She proves that entrepreneurship is not just about innovation or profit—

it's about cultivating potential, enabling others, and shaping a future where opportunity and knowledge are shared. Through her mentorship, strategic guidance, and commitment to sustainable business, Sharkey embodies the vision of *Sheconomy™ Magazine*: that the next economy is built when leaders rise together, lifting others as they lead.

www.sherisesstudios.com

ENGINEERING GENERATIONAL WEALTH THROUGH SYSTEMS, NOT SPRINTS

By **Albert Richer**
Founder WhatAreTheBest.com

Most people think generational wealth is built through money, luck, or a breakthrough event. But the longer I've been an entrepreneur, the more I've learned that those things are small contributors. The real foundation of multi-generational wealth is the creation of systems that can operate without you. Wealth grows when you stop being the bottleneck, and when the knowledge, processes, and values of the business can be transferred long after you're gone.

I run one of the largest product comparison platforms online, and that scale didn't come from brute-forcing growth—it came from building frameworks that allow the system to run consistently every day, whether I am involved or not. I learned early that there is a fundamental difference between a business that survives on the founder's effort and a business that survives because it's structurally engineered for longevity.

Entrepreneurs often fall into the trap of thinking they must make every decision, solve every issue, and hold all the knowledge. But anything that depends entirely on the founder eventually collapses under the weight of that dependency. Legacy-focused businesses take the opposite approach: they document everything, delegate effectively, and build assets that accumulate value over time. These assets might be brand trust, data, process documentation, culture, customer loyalty, or technology—but the key is that they continue compounding even when the founder steps away.

One of the most transformative shifts in my mindset came from understanding the difference between optimizing for growth and optimizing for durability. Growth is seductive; it feels fast and exciting. But durability is what lasts. A durable business can weather market cycles, leadership changes, economic downturns, and personal life events. It is predictable where growth-focused businesses are volatile. It is stable where others are fragile.

Durability always wins in the long run, and it forces you to think generationally. Instead of asking, *"How do I grow this now?"* you begin asking, *"How do I build this so it still works 20 years from now?"* That shift influences every decision: the tools you choose, the systems you design, the people you hire, and the values you codify.

Generational wealth is not just the transfer of money; it's the transfer of knowledge capital, structural capital, and a philosophy that outlasts any market cycle. Money alone gets spent. Systems, however, continue producing value indefinitely. When you build processes that can be passed down—whether to family members, future leadership, or the next generation of entrepreneurs—you create wealth that compounds beyond your lifetime.

For me, this realization helped clarify the difference between owning a job and owning a business. A job stops paying you when you stop working. A business built on durable systems continues generating results long after your direct involvement. That is the essence of generational wealth: the ability for future generations to inherit not just capital, but consistency.

Legacy isn't created by accident; it is engineered. It's built through thoughtful documentation, clear decision-making frameworks, and the willingness to decentralize control. It grows when founders invest in the infrastructure of their company as seriously as they invest in revenue. It's strengthened when you turn knowledge into processes, processes into systems, and systems into an engine that runs independent of you.

In many ways, generational wealth is the ultimate expression of responsible entrepreneurship. It means creating something that outlives your schedule, your energy, and even your lifespan. It means shifting your identity from *"operator"* to *"architect,"* and designing a structure strong enough to hold the weight of future opportunity.

If I distilled everything I've learned into one truth, it would be this:
Generational impact isn't achieved through speed—it's achieved through systems.

Sprints create momentum, but systems create legacy. And legacy is the most valuable asset any entrepreneur can pass on.

Connect With Albert

www.WhatAreTheBest.com
Email: albert@whatarethebest.com
www.linkedin.com/in/albert-r-1b267130

HOW ENTREPRENEURS BUILD BUSINESSES THAT OUTLIVE THEM

By **Joseph Petrusky**

What does it really take to build something that lasts? Not just a profitable business, but a company with staying power —one that still delivers value long after the founder is gone.

For entrepreneurs, investors, and family business leaders, legacy isn't about ego. It's about sustainability, succession, and stewardship. A business that outlives its founder isn't built by chance. It's built with structure, values, and long-term thinking.

Here's how founders can shift from short-term gains to long-term legacy.

Think Beyond the Exit

Most startups are built for a sale. That's fine for investors chasing fast ROI, but it won't build generational impact. Sustainable businesses aren't built just to sell—they're built to last. That means investing in people, systems, and culture instead of just profit margins.

For instance, cash homebuyer companies that want to stay relevant through market cycles can't rely on the founder's hustle alone. They need systems that work with or without the original owner. This applies whether you're buying five homes a year or 500.

If your business needs you in every room and every decision, it's not built to outlive you.

Start by designing yourself out of the day-to-day. Build processes that others can run. Delegate leadership early. Don't just hire for tasks. Hire future leaders who can make decisions without you.

Document Everything. Then Improve It.

Every business that survives long-term runs on repeatable systems. Not talent. Not hustle. Not the founder's charm. Systems.

Make documentation a daily discipline. Your best team member should be able to leave, and a new hire should be able to take over without a massive learning curve. That only works if everything—from how you close deals to how you onboard clients—is written down, refined, and repeatable.

The more consistent your operations, the more valuable, and sustainable, your company becomes.

Values First, Always

What you stand for matters more than what you sell.

Sustainable companies are built on clear values. They aren't buried in a mission statement. They're practicing. They're enforced. And they're used to making hard decisions.

Leaders who create lasting impact define those values early, communicate them often, and model them consistently.

If your company stands for *"speed,"* then internal processes should prioritize responsiveness. If your brand is about *"trust,"* then customer interactions must be transparent and honest.

Values protect a company when leadership changes. They become the true foundation for long-term culture.

Build Around Real People, Not Just Profit

People-first companies last longer. Period.

That means treating employees like long-term partners, not disposable labor. It also means knowing your customers deeply—not just their wallets, but their motivations.

Customers stick with companies that know them. Employees stay with leaders who invest in them. Loyalty is built through real connection, not quarterly bonuses.

Founders who build community inside and outside the business create stronger roots. Those roots matter when it's time to pass the company on.

Don't Wait for Succession—Start It Now

Succession isn't a retirement plan. It's a growth strategy.

Start identifying future leaders from day one. Share financials. Teach decision-making. Let others lead meetings, solve problems, and drive change.

When it's time to step away, there should already be leaders in place who think like owners and act like stewards.

Waiting until *"someday"* to plan for succession almost guarantees a rushed, reactive transition. Start now—even if you're nowhere near ready to leave.

Final Thought: Legacy Is a Choice

Building a business that outlives you doesn't happen by accident. It's intentional. It's methodical. And it requires leaders to act with long-term discipline even when short-term gains are tempting.

If you're an entrepreneur looking to make a real impact, think beyond yourself. Build for the next generation. And start now.

Connect With Joseph

www.schuylkillhome.com

100
WOMEN OF IMPACT™
THE DOCUSERIES THAT AMPLIFIES WOMEN'S VOICES

We just wrapped our first taping of 100 Women of Impact™ in San Diego, and the momentum has only just begun. This powerful docuseries is shining a spotlight on extraordinary women who are shaping the future through leadership, resilience, and influence.

Be part of the movement by sharing your story in an exclusive filmed interview for the docuseries. Gain visibility through red carpet experiences, media coverage, and distribution across She Rises Studios platforms, while connecting with a global network of women making an unstoppable impact.

NEXT FILMING OPPORTUNITIES

SHE WINS GLOBAL SUMMIT | LAS VEGAS | NOVEMBER 6–7, 2025
EMPOWERHER CONTENT DAY | LAS VEGAS | FEBRUARY 2026

SIGN UP TODAY

VISIT WWW.SHERISESSTUDIOS.COM/INTRODUCING-100-WOMEN-OF-IMPACT TO CLAIM YOUR SPOT.

ENROLL FREE TODAY TO SCALE YOUR BUSINESS

She Rises Studios and Goldman Sachs 10,000 Women join forces to provide education, resources, and a supportive global community for women-led SMEs, empowering them to grow, innovate, and thrive in today's competitive landscape.

UNIVERSITY OF LEEDS

Goldman Sachs 10,000 WOMEN

SHE RISES STUDIOS

BUILDING LEGACY THROUGH LEADERSHIP:
HOW ENTREPRENEURS CREATE BUSINESSES THAT OUTLIVE THEM

By **Briana Marie Riley**
Founder, 1 Million CEOs™

As an entrepreneur and the founder of the 1 Million CEOs™ movement, I often say that building a business is bigger than income - it's about IMPACT. And that is why my mission is to help moms all over the world step into the role of CEO in their lives, their families, and their communities to create true generational wealth.

To me, legacy is not something we just leave behind; it's something that we must build *intentionally*. And when entrepreneurs truly embrace that CEO mindset, their businesses and the wisdom they share will quite naturally outlive them.

Let's dive deeper into this.

How Entrepreneurs Can Create Businesses That Outlive Them

A business becomes generational when it is designed with systems, not just personal effort. Far too many founders build companies that depend completely on their own energy, creativity, or presence. And that model simply cannot be passed down. Longevity requires *structure*.

There are three things I encourage every CEO in my community to focus on:

Documentation and Systems

A legacy-driven business is one where the *"how"* is written down, not just kept in the founder's mind. Standard operating procedures, brand guidelines, values, and decision-making frameworks are all tools that allow the mission to survive even when the founder steps back. Systems create stability, and stability creates lifespan.

An Empowered Leadership Ecosystem

If you are the only leader, the business *cannot* outlive you. But when you intentionally develop a culture where leadership is distributed and where team members understand the mission, feel ownership, and are empowered to innovate, you create a company that can grow beyond your lifespan. Your people become the carriers of your vision.

A Mission Bigger Than the Founder

When the purpose is tied only to the founder's personal story, it has a natural end date. But when the purpose speaks to community transformation, industry innovation, or generational change, it becomes timeless.

For example, the 1 Million CEOs™ movement exists far beyond me; it exists to shift how women and our children see themselves and what they believe they are capable of. That purpose can be carried forward indefinitely.

Legacy vs. Short-Term Gain

One of the biggest lessons I've learned is that chasing quick wins can cost you long-term wealth both financially and spiritually. Short-term moves are often rooted in ego: visibility, fast sales, rapid growth, instant validation. But legacy requires restraint. It requires making strategic decisions that may not pay off today, but will create exponential impact years from now.

I have learned to ask myself one question before making major moves: ***Does this serve the next generation of this business?*** If not, it's a distraction.

Legacy is built through consistency, alignment, and strategic patience.

Defining Wealth Beyond Money

For me, wealth is freedom, influence, and generational elevation.

- **Freedom** is the ability to make choices based on values rather than survival. It is the space to create without panic and to lead without desperation.
- **Influence** is the power to open doors, shift narratives, and change how our communities see themselves. Wealth becomes legacy when your influence continues to uplift others long after you're gone.
- **Generational elevation** is the most meaningful wealth of all. It is when your children and their children and their community inherit not just resources, but belief systems, standards, and opportunities that position them to lead even better than you did.

Money is ultimately just a tool. Legacy is a mission. And true wealth is the ripple effect of a life and business built with intention.

Through the 1 Million CEOs™ movement, my work is centered on helping women become builders of legacy. It is for women who create systems, opportunities, and wealth that extend far beyond their lifetime. That, to me, is the ultimate success.

Connect With Briana

www.majorleaguemommy.com/1-million-ceos
www.instagram.com/brianamarieceo
www.linkedin.com/in/brianariley

WHY YOUR LEGACY ISN'T ABOUT WEALTH —IT'S ABOUT WHO YOU LEAVE BEHIND

By **Alex Mason**

Here's a statistic that should make every wealth-builder pause: 70 percent of wealthy families lose their wealth by the second generation, and a staggering 90 percent lose it by the third [1]. Meanwhile, Ramsey Solutions' National Study of Millionaires found that 79 percent of millionaires didn't receive any inheritance at all [2]. These numbers tell us something profound: wealth doesn't perpetuate itself. But more importantly, they invite a deeper question—if money doesn't last, what does?

What the Wealthy Learn Too Late

When billionaires reflect on their lives, a common theme emerges. Many regret working so hard and wish they had invested more in the people around them [3]. Warren Buffett has said, "*Success is really about being in balance with the people who matter most to you*" [4]. Bill Gates acknowledged regretting his previous workaholic lifestyle, telling graduates, "*Don't wait as long as I did to learn this lesson. Take time to nurture your relationships*" [5]. These aren't idle reflections. These are hard-won insights from people who achieved extraordinary financial success and discovered its limitations. No amount of wealth could buy back the dinners missed, the conversations cut short, or the friendships left to wither. Time, once spent, is gone forever.

The Currency of Experience

Life experiences derive their meaning from being shared. The trip with old friends, the long conversation over coffee, the quiet evening with someone you love—these moments aren't distractions from building wealth. They are wealth in its most valid form. They shape who we are, deepen our connections, and create the memories that define a life well-lived.

Research consistently shows that experiences bring more lasting happiness than material purchases. Objects depreciate; memories appreciate. The vacation you took ten years ago likely means more to you now than it did then. The relationships you've cultivated over decades become richer with each passing year.

Relationships as the Foundation

The Harvard Study of Adult Development, one of the longest studies on human happiness, followed participants for over 80 years. Its conclusion was simple but profound: good relationships keep us happier and healthier.

Not wealth. Not fame. Not achievement. Relationships. The people who fared best were those who leaned into connections with family, friends, and community.

Yet in the pursuit of financial success, relationships are often the first casualty. We tell ourselves we'll reconnect later, after the next milestone, after the business stabilizes. But later has a way of never arriving. The relationships that matter require presence, and presence requires time—the one resource that wealth cannot replenish.

Preparing Those You Leave Behind

When families fail to discuss wealth openly—and studies show 64 percent disclose little to nothing about their finances to loved ones—they leave the next generation unprepared [1]. But the real preparation isn't about money management. It's about transmitting values, sharing wisdom, and modeling what a meaningful life looks like. The conversations we have, the examples we set, and the time we invest in others—these are the true inheritance.

The True Legacy

A legacy isn't measured in net worth. It's measured in the depth of your relationships, the experiences you've shared, and the lives you've touched. It's the friend who still calls you after thirty years. It's the family traditions that outlive you. It's the values that echo through generations long after the money is spent.

In the end, the greatest gift you can give isn't financial—it's your time, your attention, and your presence. That's the legacy worth building.

Connect With Alex

www.linkedin.com/in/jalexmason

she wins

WOMEN'S NETWORK

Elevate your business with the power of community.

Get access to the tools, connections, and support you need to grow—with a circle of women who truly get it.

WHAT'S INCLUDED

- Strategic networking & mentorship
- Expert-led masterclasses & exclusive resources
- Member spotlights, VIP perks & more

Join for just

$87/MONTH

no contracts, cancel anytime.

www.shewinswomensnetwork.com

INSPIRE
EMPOWER
EDUCATE

BUILDING SUSTAINABLE SUCCESS ACROSS GENERATIONS: INTENT IS IRRELEVANT

By **Cecily Welch, CPA, CFP®, PFS**
The Accountant You Can Understand ®

You've probably heard the saying, *"The road to hell is paved with good intentions."* When it comes to family wealth and business succession, the same principle applies. Matriarchs and patriarchs often express heartfelt wishes—passing down the family business, ensuring success for their children, and creating a lasting legacy. But without a written plan aligned with current (tax) laws and the guidance of professional advisors, those intentions rarely translate into reality. Too often, a thriving business for one generation becomes a failed experiment for the next.

Why Intent Alone Fails

Intent doesn't override operating agreements, beneficiary forms, state intestate laws (dying without a will), or a written will. Intent also doesn't resolve family disputes. Further, a business that depends entirely on its founder will die when they do. Sustainable success requires systems, scalability, and structure—none of which happen by accident.

Professional advisors aren't a cost center; they're an investment by creating frameworks, including:
- Buy/Sell Agreements and Compensation Structures for family members who work in the business and for those who don't.
- Clear On and Off Ramps for family participation and ownership.
- Retention Incentives for key employees who are critical to continuity.
- Documents that comply with state and federal tax laws to minimize transfer taxes, capital gains, and tools for resolving conflicts.
- Ensuring pathways exist for succession (i.e. law firms can only be passed on to other lawyers)

Planning Beyond Paperwork

True multi-generational planning requires understanding people, anticipating change, and non-intuitive considerations such as:
- **Individualized Strategies:** Treating children equally doesn't mean treating them the same. Succession planning should reflect each child's strengths, interests, and abilities.
- **Conversations:** Replace dictation with dialogue. Encourage family members to be self-centered. Yes, you read that right.

Selfish is trying to get what you want regardless of other people. Self-centered means advocating for what you need and want. Through honest sharing of needs and wants, there's an increased likelihood of successful transitions.
- **Independent Advisor Relationships:** Allow children to build trust with family advisors separate from their parents. Yes, sometimes this means the parent paying for separate engagements for their children.
- **Communication:** Share long-term plans with key employees to maintain loyalty and stability.
- **Future-Proofing:** Discuss what *"family"* means in your plan. Consider adopted children, stepchildren, remarried spouses, etc.

Flexibility Is Possible

Many business owners hesitate to formalize plans, fearing permanence. In reality, most structures allow for amendments when circumstances change. But if you don't create a plan, the state will—and its version rarely aligns with your goals. Anyone wishing to have financial independence ignores taxes at their peril. And rules regarding wealth transfer are constantly changing – requiring frequent updates. Unfortunately, no, the old strategy of set it and forget it is no longer possible for taxes and estate law (yes – you will have an estate when you die – 'estate' isn't reserved for the wealthy - you may not have estate tax, but that doesn't mean you don't have an estate)

Of course it's about the money – but why?

Wealth is about choices. Building a legacy means respecting that your family's choices may differ from yours. Remember: earning wealth requires different skills than maintaining it and thus consider education, opportunities, learning curves and pathways for the next generation to learn and lead. And maybe, find outside success while still maintaining ownership.

The Bottom Line

Intent is irrelevant without action. Sustainable success demands written plans, professional guidance, and ongoing communication. If you want your business and wealth to outlast you, start today—because doing nothing is still a plan, and it's the state's plan, not yours.

Connect With Cecily

www.cecilywelch.cpa
www.linkedin.com/in/cecilywelch
www.facebook.com/CecilyWelchCPA
www.instagram.com/cecilywelchcpa
www.x.com/cecilywelchcpa

BUILDING A LEGACY THROUGH PURPOSE, LEADERSHIP, AND SERVICE

By **Krystle Phillips**

Legacy, to me, is not a monument you build at the end of your life. It's the trail of impact you leave every day, intentionally, quietly, and consistently, long before anyone calls it a legacy. I grew up in Trinidad, in a small community where resources were limited but resilience was abundant. That environment taught me early on that legacy isn't built through titles or visibility, but through the lives you touch when no one is keeping score.

Today, as the founder of YES (Your Equipment Suppliers) and two additional brands serving entrepreneurs across the Caribbean and diaspora, I define my legacy in simple terms: **access, opportunity, and upward mobility for people who were never supposed to have it**.

My companies were never built to simply sell equipment or products. They exist to level the playing field for small and mid-sized founders. People with talent and ambition, but limited capital, little technical guidance, and no clear roadmap. For more than a decade, my work has been driven by one central question: *How do I make it easier for someone else to rise than it was for me?*

Every operational system, every training program, every after-sales support structure is tied back to that purpose. That is how I build my legacy—through service that outlives the transaction.

A turning point in my life reshaped not only how I lead, but who I lead for. Several years ago, while running multiple companies, I became the full-time caregiver for my mother. Overnight, the identity I had built, strong, independent, relentlessly capable, collided with the reality of caregiving, burnout, and emotional exhaustion. It forced me to confront questions I had long avoided: *What does leadership look like when you can't hold everything together? What happens when strength stops working?*

One day, in the middle of that season, someone casually asked how business was going. For the first time, I didn't default to a polished answer. I said, *"I'm barely holding it together."* That honesty cracked something open. I realized leadership isn't about holding the world up alone. It's about allowing others to hold pieces of it with you.

That realization changed everything: how I built my team, how I designed systems, and how I showed up for the entrepreneurs who trusted my companies for guidance.

Caregiving taught me a leadership principle that now shapes every decision I make: **you cannot pour into others from a place of depletion**. Sustainable service requires sustainable structure. From that point forward, I stopped romanticizing silent strength and began building businesses rooted in clarity, support, and shared responsibility.

Sustainable, values-driven leadership, in my experience, rests on three core principles.

First, purpose must precede profit.
When your mission is clear and your values are non-negotiable, profit becomes a by-product of trust. People can feel the difference between a company that sells to them and one that walks with them.

Second, systems protect what passion builds.
Burnout happens when purpose has no infrastructure. Legacy cannot depend on one person's energy; it must be supported by processes, documentation, and teams that allow impact to scale beyond the founder.

Third, leadership is service with boundaries.
Availability is not effectiveness. Clear expectations, communication, and boundaries don't weaken leadership. They strengthen it. When leaders protect their energy, they create healthier cultures and more resilient teams.

Today, the entrepreneurs we support are not just customers; they are future legacy builders themselves. Every time someone uses our guidance to open a shop, expand a menu, hire their first employee, or gain confidence in their craft, that is legacy, not mine alone, but ours.

I'm building a legacy that says this: *a Caribbean woman chose to lead with purpose, built access where none existed, and helped thousands rise without losing themselves in the process.*

That is the story I intend to leave behind.

Connect With Krystle

www.krystlephillips.com
www.rollicecream.com
www.yourequipmentsuppliers.com
@trinikrystle

THE ULTIMATE SUPERFOOD FOR DOGS

SUPPORTS JOINT HEALTH FOR DOGS OF ALL AGES

Fortified with Vet-Recommended servings of glucosamine and chondroitin

NATURALLY RICH IN COLLAGEN

And infused with Omegas 3, 6, and 9 for Skin & Coat Health

FLAVOR BOOST FOR MEALS

Boosts flavor at mealtime - just a splash over meals has even the pickiest pups licking their bowls clean.

AIDS IN DIGESTION

Supports natural detoxification of the gut and is gentle on sensitive stomachs.

BRUTUSBROTH.COM

Non-Alcoholic Cocktails

SHOP NOW I DRINKTILDEN.COM

BUILDING A LEGACY THROUGH PURPOSE, LEADERSHIP, AND SERVICE

By **Annika La Vina**

When I first stepped into this role, I thought my job was to become the best founder I could be — sharp, fast, decisive, and ultimately commercial. But branching into the defense vertical within my dual-use company opened my eyes to an entirely different kind of responsibility.

Commercial readiness is one thing. National security — where failure could mean civilian loss of life — demands something else entirely. I had to shift from building a *"product"* to deeply solving a problem that cannot afford to be wrong. That shift forced me to level up, not just as a CEO, but as someone accountable to outcomes beyond financials.

In dual-use companies, you can't just move fast. You have to move fast and correctly. It becomes existential. Your judgment carries real-world consequences. Your roadmap isn't just a strategy — it's a statement of what you believe should exist in the world.

Legacy, to me, is the imprint you leave through decisions made under pressure — especially when no one is watching. It's not just product-market fit. It's problem-mission fit. That turning point came when I stopped asking, *"How do we win this market?"* and started asking, *"What must exist — because lives depend on it?"*

The principles that ground me are these:
- **Service above ego** — The mission must outlive the founder.
- **Clarity over charisma** — People don't need to be dazzled; they need to be led.
- **Resolve through chaos** — True leadership reveals itself when things go wrong, not right.

Legacy isn't just the company you build — it's the discipline and duty you model for everyone who follows. And for me, that means building not just for traction, but for trust. Not just for users, but for safety. Not just for success — but for service.

Connect With Annika

www.dracointelligence.com
www.dracointelligence.com/annikalavina
www.linkedin.com/in/annikalavina

DOTTIE ROSE
F O U N D A T I O N®

Our mission is to set the standard in computer science education while bridging the gender gap in the technology field.

We envision a future where computer science education is accessible, inclusive, and equitable for all, regardless of gender and a technology industry that values and benefits from the diverse perspectives and contributions of women.

Located Charlotte, NC | **Serving** North Carolina • South Carolina • Floridia • International

LEARN MORE I DOTTIEROSEFOUNDATION.ORG

REDEFINING LEGACY:
BUILDING A FUTURE THAT BREAKS CYCLES, NOT SPIRITS

By **Victoria Barkow**

When people talk about *"legacy,"* they usually picture something polished and far-off: money in a trust, a name on a building, a perfectly mapped-out future for generations. But for many of us, legacy starts in the everyday choices we make, the habits we unlearn, and the beliefs we refuse to pass down.

For me, legacy is simple and deeply personal: raising my children to be self-dependent in an ever-changing world and breaking the generational poverty mindset that's lingered for far too long.

Money isn't just a tool for personal comfort - it's a force that can transform families, empower communities, and rewrite stories. Financial stability expands possibilities. It creates space for creativity, safety, choice, and dignity. And when you grow up in a community where money was scarce or feared or mishandled, you realize just how powerful it is to flip that narrative.

My legacy starts with building something of my own - my business, my path, my proof that a different future is possible. Entrepreneurship becomes more than a career; it becomes an act of defiance against the limits others accepted. It becomes a model for my children: this is what it looks like to choose growth over excuses, confidence over scarcity, and vision over fear.

The Moment Everything Shifted

We all have that one moment that quietly - sometimes not so quietly - reshapes the way we show up for others.

For me, that moment came when I realized something both simple and powerful: people respond to honesty and clarity far more than they respond to sugarcoating.

For so long, I thought kindness meant cushioning the truth. I believed that being supportive meant softening the message so no one felt uncomfortable. But I learned quickly that clarity is the real form of respect. People don't grow in confusion. They don't thrive with half-answers. And they absolutely don't become their strongest selves when everything is packaged to sound *"nice."*

Once I embraced directness - with compassion, not sharpness - everything changed. My conversations became more meaningful. My leadership became more effective. People trusted me more because they never had to guess what I meant.

Leadership isn't about pleasing everyone.

It's about serving people in a way that actually moves them forward. And real service requires real honesty.

Leadership That Lasts Requires Thinking Beyond the Surface

Values-driven leadership sounds great, but few people talk about what it actually *requires*. For me, it boils down to one core skill: critical thinking.

Sustainable leadership means acknowledging that every decision has layers - ripples that extend far beyond the moment it's made. When you choose a direction, you're not just affecting the next step; you're shaping the next several outcomes, opportunities, and obstacles.

Surface-level decisions might keep the peace in the moment, but they rarely build anything that lasts. The real work is looking deeper:

- *How will this decision affect the team two months from now?*
- *What message does it send about our values?*
- *Does this choice align with the legacy we're trying to build?*
- *Am I choosing convenience or integrity?*

Values matter because they ground us. They help us sleep at night. They define the kind of leaders, parents, partners, and people we want to be. But values aren't just slogans; they require action. They require thought. They require responsibility.

And that responsibility is the heart of leadership.
Legacy isn't built in the future - it's built now.

It's built in the way you raise your children, the beliefs you challenge, the business you create, and the honesty you offer the world.

It's built in your willingness to think deeper, lead clearer, and live bolder.

Everything else?
That's just the story people tell later.

I THOUGHT BEING A GREAT LEADER MEANT EVERYONE KNEW MY NAME.

By **Maria Rosey**
Founder of one touch finance

I thought being a great leader meant everyone knew my name. Then I met Jennifer. Here's the embarrassing truth: I spent years building the wrong thing. Have you ever had one of those moments where you realize you've been doing everything backward? Yeah. That was me on a Tuesday afternoon.

I'm sitting there looking at this shiny award on my desk. My name's engraved on it. We just crushed this massive project. I should feel amazing, right? But when I walked through the office that morning, my team looked dead inside. No high-fives. No excitement. Just people who couldn't wait to go home. And I'm sitting there thinking: What did I actually win here?

The moment everything clicked

Jennifer was one of my best team members. Super talented. Always delivered. One day, she comes into my office and quits. I'm shocked. "*But we're doing so well! Look at what we've accomplished!*" She looks at me and says something I'll never forget: "*You've accomplished a lot. I've just been helping you do it.*"

Ouch. She wasn't wrong. I'd been so busy building the reputation that I forgot to help anyone else build theirs. That's when I got it. Legacy isn't about you being remembered. It's about what keeps going after you leave.

What I thought legacy meant (spoiler: I was super wrong)

Before Jennifer quit, I thought legacy was pretty simple:

Your name on stuff. Awards. Being "*that person who did that thing.*" But that's not legacy. That's just ego with better marketing. Real legacy? It's when someone says, "*They helped me become who I am.*" It's when the good stuff keeps happening even after you're gone.

Think about your favorite teacher. You probably don't remember every single lesson. But you remember how they made you feel capable. How they saw something in you that you didn't see yet. That's the stuff that matters.

What changed after Jennifer left

I did something I'd never done before. I called a team meeting and asked: "*What do you actually need from me?*" Nobody talked at first. It was awkward. Then people started being honest:

- "*I need you to listen to my ideas, not just tell me yours.*"
- "*I need time to actually learn new things, not just crank out work.*"
- "*I need to feel like this is OUR thing, not YOUR thing that I'm helping with.*"

Man, that hurt to hear. But they were right. I'd been the bottleneck. The person in the way. Not the person helping people grow. So I changed my main question from "*How do I make a bigger impact?*" to "Who am I helping become better?" Everything got different after that.

The stuff I actually care about now

Here's what I figured out: You can't build anything that lasts by yourself. Impossible. Will you be proud of HOW you did this? I started asking myself this before every big decision: "*Would I feel good explaining this choice to myself in five years?*" If the answer is no, I don't do it. Simple as that.

Like, yeah, I could push my team to work weekends and hit the deadline. But would I be proud of that? Nope. Your values only count when they're hard. Anyone can say they believe in something. But do you believe it when it costs you? I said I cared about work-life balance. But I kept scheduling 7 pm calls. My actions were saying something totally different. Now I ask: "*What am I willing to lose for this value?*" If the answer is nothing, then it's not really a value. It's just nice words.

Give away your best stuff

This sounds weird, but hear me out. I used to keep my best ideas and opportunities for myself. Made sense, right? That's how you get ahead. Wrong. When you hoard everything, you become the limit. You're the ceiling everyone hits. But when you give stuff away? When you teach people everything you know? When you recommend someone else for the cool opportunity? They grow. They win. And then they bring all that new knowledge back and make everyone better. You're not the hero anymore. You're the person who makes heroes. That's way more powerful.

Talk less, listen way more

I used to think being a leader meant having all the answers. Now I know it means asking better questions and actually listening. Try this: Next conversation you have, try to listen 70% of the time. It feels super weird at first. But you'll hear things you've been missing forever. The best ideas aren't in your head. They're in the heads of the people actually doing the work.

What I'm building instead

My legacy isn't a title or a building anymore. It's people. It's the person who got promoted because I spent time helping them grow. It's the leader who told me, "*You showed me there's a different way to do this.*" It's knowing that when I move on, the team will keep being awesome without me.

Want to know if you're building something real? Look around you. Are people better because of you? Not just more productive. Actually BETTER. More confident. More skilled. More themselves. That's how you know.

Here's what I want you to do

Stop thinking about what people will remember about you. Start thinking about whom you're helping become someone worth remembering. Ask yourself this week:

- Who did I help grow?
- What did I give away that made someone else stronger?
- Am I making space for others, or am I taking up all the oxygen?

Legacy isn't something you build alone and leave behind like a monument. It's something you build THROUGH people. And it keeps growing long after you're gone. That Tuesday when I stared at my award and saw my exhausted team? That changed me. I stopped chasing my name on things. Started investing in people whose names would never be next to mine. And honestly? This feels a million times better than any award ever did.

So what's your moment going to be? When are you going to stop building for yourself and start building for them?

Connect With Maria

www.onetouchfinance.com

THE LEGACY OF BEING STUBBORN AS F♥CK

By **Adriana L. Cowdin**

For most of my life, I believed legacy was built through hustle, titles, and relentless ambition, until my body, my life, and my purpose forced me to rewrite the story entirely.

I was the woman who outworked everyone. The first in, the last out. I had senior executive roles in Fortune 500 companies, was a successful entrepreneur, won prestigious awards, and had the luxury lifestyle that it afforded. Hustle gave me power, independence, and results. Or did it?

One thing I know for sure is it nearly cost me everything.

In my 30s and 40s, I was climbing the corporate ladder at a pace that people train for an Ironman. Obsessively. Compulsively. Sacrificing everything else for the next milestone.

And then my body pulled a hostile takeover on me. One day I was running the show and the next I was being dragged to the boardroom of survival. Literally.

In 2016, I spent more time in the hospital than I did at home. I was fighting for my life, living on feeding tubes to nourish my skeletal body, narcotics to make the pain bearable, and nausea meds to stop the vomiting. Within the last decade, I've had dozens of surgeries, including the Whipple (if you want to lose your appetite, Google it). They've removed my pancreas, two-thirds of my stomach, my gallbladder, most of my small intestines, and done a cell transplant into my liver.

By 2025, I'd been diagnosed with more than 30 chronic conditions—Chronic Pancreatitis, Lupus, Addison's, Diabetes, and liver disease. Illness didn't knock politely; it bulldozed everything.

I've survived multiple code blues. I've said goodbye to my best friend, my favorite person in the world, my husband, Eric. These moments have a way of reminding you that titles, awards, and luxury goods mean nothing when it comes to real legacy.

I had to face the question: If this is it… what did it all mean?

That reckoning gave birth to my book: *Stubborn As F♥ck: 13 Certain Truths to Rise, Reclaim, and Reinvent Your Life*. The 13 Certain Truths in *SAF* are real, lived truths.

Eric and I met mere months before my body broke down and rewrote our life plans. This incredible man who fell in love with a polished executive loved me even with my broken body and far less predictable life. He didn't love my title, bank account, or lifestyle. He loved me.

He's the reason I'm still alive. That, and I'm too damn stubborn to die. I was given a 25% chance to live until 2021. Here I am, still fighting. I won't pretend it's easy. I live on a feeding tube. My organs (what's left of them) don't work. Getting out of bed is a conscious decision. But I'm a fighter and that's the legacy I've chosen to leave behind, through this book and the movement it's launched.

I didn't write *Stubborn As F♥ck* to inspire the masses. I wrote it to reach one person. The one barely holding it together who reads my story and thinks, *"If she can wake up with resilience and gratitude, maybe I can too."*

Legacy is built in the moments no one claps for. When you make someone feel seen. When you give them permission to exhale. When you show up with grace instead of ego. That's the legacy I'm building now, one stubborn, honest day at a time. And it's not just my legacy anymore. It's our, mine and Eric's.

My legacy is how I live today, in this body, with the people who matter.

Connect With Adriana

www.adrianacowdin.com
www.instagram.com/adrianalcowdin
www.linkedin.com/in/adrianacowdin
www.facebook.com/adriana.cowdin.2025

SHOP NOW I FUNCHO.CO

HARO connects journalists with sources for stories.

Journalists, submit a query to connect with sources.

SUBSCRIBE FOR FREE DAILY MEDIA QUERIES.

WWW.HELPAREPORTER.COM

LEGACY IS BUILT IN MOTION, NOT AT THE FINISH LINE

By **Alexandra Aileru**
Founder of Confident Career Switch

Legacy is often framed as something we consider at the end of a career. But what if legacy is something we build continuously—through the way we serve, lead, and evolve over time?

For many professionals, career change feels daunting not because they lack ability, but because they struggle to see how their impact carries forward. Career pivots are often misinterpreted as starting over, when in reality they are opportunities to serve more people, more effectively. The greater the number of people you serve—and the more intentional you are about *how* you serve—the deeper your long-term impact becomes.

This shift begins with identity, not job titles. Long-term impact is shaped by who you choose to become, not simply what role you hold. You must be it first, then do it, then have it.

My own career journey—from high school teacher, to corporate project manager, to full-time entrepreneur—forced me to redefine success on my own terms. Each transition required an internal reckoning: reassessing my values, letting go of external definitions of achievement, and choosing to show up as a person aligned with what truly mattered to me.

When I didn't do this, I experienced burnout—masking who I was to fit roles that no longer aligned. That disconnect didn't just affect me; it limited how effectively I could serve others. True success, I learned, is not about meeting the world's expectations, but about becoming the person you were designed to be.

Today, as the founder of Confident Career Switch, I help mid-career professionals—especially women—navigate career transitions through this same values-driven, identity-first approach. I don't just help people change jobs; I help them realign who they are with how they work and lead. This is the foundation of sustainable, meaningful leadership.

My guiding principle is simple: leadership and service must always start internally.

When you know and honor your values, career pivots become clearer, impact becomes scalable, and legacy becomes something you live—not something you leave behind.

If you're questioning your next chapter, start with identity. The career will follow.

To explore how identity-led career transitions create long-term impact, connect with Confident Career Switch.

Connect With Alexandra

www.confidentcareerswitch.com

LEGACY BEGINS IN CHILDHOOD:

REIMAGINING SERVICE, LEADERSHIP, AND THE COMMUNITIES OUR CHILDREN WILL INHERIT

By **Raquel Whiting Gilmer**
Founder & CEO, Perfectly Me

When people talk about legacy, they often think in terms of accomplishments made over a lifetime. A career or awards won. A reputation that endures long after you're gone.

For me, legacy is something deeper. It's the values we plant in children long before they become adults. It's the belief that who they are has the power to shape the world around them.

My legacy isn't a single achievement. It's a movement, one child at a time, toward a more compassionate, courageous, community-minded generation.

I came to this work through the lessons passed down from my great-grandmother that no matter how little we have, we always have something to give. Service and community were paramount for me as a child despite our limited financial resources. This became the seed of Perfectly Me, the mission-driven company I founded to help children build the values I wish someone had helped me build and nurture when I was young.

What started as programming for camps and clubs to instill these values, has become something bigger. We're cultivating the next generation of citizens. Children who understand kindness as a civic skill, empathy as a responsibility, and service as part of their identity.

The turning point that reshaped how I lead came from my own son, Mikey. When he was six, we were walking by a local park and he noticed trash on the ground. He didn't complain. He simply said, "*There aren't enough trash cans.*"

For him, this wasn't just an observation. *It was the beginning of a plan.*

He organized a cleanup. He recruited friends. He asked neighbors for help. What began as one child's idea grew into a six-year operation that now has a 30-person community effort supported by local partners. As his mother, I had to make a choice: treat this as a cute childhood moment, or honor it as the early formation of citizenship. I chose the latter. That choice changed me.

Mikey's story reminded me that children are naturally wired for impact. They just need adults who are willing to pause and support. Parents often talk about raising leaders, but leadership is formed in the small moments when a child notices a problem and an adult helps them believe they can be part of the solution.

This is why I believe it's time to reconsider the concept of "*community service requirements.*" For too long, service has been something we require children to log rather than something we help them embody. Hours don't change culture. Identity does.

At Perfectly Me, we don't count hours. We cultivate values. We create programs and experiences where children practice courage, kindness, leadership, and community commitment until those behaviors become part of who they are.

That shift, from compliance to identity, is the heart of my leadership philosophy, which rests on a few simple principles:

1. Identity before action.
People act in alignment with who they believe themselves to be. When children see themselves as contributors and problem-solvers, their actions naturally follow.

2. Service is learned through experience, not instruction.
No worksheet can teach empathy. No policy can create compassion. Children learn values by living them.

3. Community is built, not assumed.
Teaching our children how to create community, not just exist within it, is a leadership skill we cannot afford to overlook in today's culture.

4. Legacy is not what we leave behind. It's what we build into others.
Every child who discovers their courage, strengthens their empathy, or leads a moment of community connection becomes a living extension of our legacy.

My hope is that when people look back on my work, they don't see camps and programs. I want them to see a generation of children who grew up believing they mattered, and who made the world better because of it.

That is the legacy I am building. And it begins in childhood.

Connect With Raquel

www.linkedin.com/in/raquelwhitinggilmer
www.perfectlyme.com

SHE RISES STUDIOS

Live Tour

10 CITIES. 2 WEEKS. EMPOWERING WOMEN EVERYWHERE.

JANUARY **12-26**   REGISTER NOW

JANUARY 30, 2026 I 11:00AM– 2:00PM PST
UP YOUR ENERGY
Summit
RISE, LEAD, AND LIGHT UP YOUR LIFE
SHE RISES STUDIOS
FENIX TV

LEGACY IS THE LEADERSHIP WE PRACTICE WHEN NO ONE IS APPLAUDING

By **Christina Bedal, SPHR**

In a world obsessed with speed, scale, and visibility, the word *legacy* is often misused if it's even understood at all. It gets reduced to milestones, metrics, or personal branding. But real legacy is not built in public moments or polished narratives. It is built quietly—through the everyday decisions leaders make long before anyone labels them influential.

Legacy, to me, is the invisible trail leaders leave behind in people, systems, and cultures. It shows up in what becomes normalized, what is tolerated, and what is modeled. It is the emotional and psychological residue of leadership—the way people experience work, power, accountability, and trust because of us. All of which are increasingly more important in the current workplace.

The uncomfortable truth is this: **legacy is being formed whether we are intentional about it or not.** The only real choice leaders have is whether that legacy is accidental or deliberate.

The most meaningful turning point for many leaders isn't dramatic or celebratory. It's the quiet realization that leadership is always teaching—especially when no one thinks they're watching.
How problems are escalated.
How conflict is handled.
How pressure is absorbed or passed down.
How mistakes are addressed.
How people are treated when they disagree or struggle.

This is where leadership shifts from execution to stewardship.

Through my work in leadership development, I see this pattern repeatedly: leaders underestimate the ecosystem effect of their behavior. Every interaction creates a deposit or a withdrawal—of trust, clarity, safety, or credibility. Over time, those transactions compound. They become patterns. And those patterns become a leader's legacy.

Legacy is not a future reflection but rather a real-time accumulation. Think of it as your leadership credit score or balance sheet, updated daily.

Sustainable, values-driven leadership doesn't rely on charisma or control. It relies on principles that hold under pressure—principles that shape how leaders behave when outcomes are uncertain and stakes are high.

First, values must cost something. If values never require discomfort, restraint, or hard conversations, they aren't values—they're preferences. Real values demand consistency even when it's inconvenient or unpopular.

Second, accountability must be human. Accountability is not punishment; it's stewardship. When used well, it protects standards while preserving dignity. It signals that growth matters more than blame.

Third, influence should be multiplied, not hoarded. Leadership that creates dependence may feel powerful in the short term, but it erodes resilience. Sustainable leaders build capability, confidence, and judgment in others. The success of others reflects us and our leadership.

Fourth, psychological safety is not optional. In modern workplaces defined by complexity, burnout, and rapid change, safety is strategic. Without it, people withhold ideas, avoid risk, and protect themselves instead of the work.

Finally, self-regulation matters more than self-sacrifice. Leaders who do not manage their internal landscape export stress, volatility, and fear. Legacy grows when leaders model emotional responsibility, not emotional suppression.

Why does intentional legacy matter now? Because the old leadership scripts are failing. People no longer want authority without awareness or productivity without humanity. They want leaders who understand that how work feels is as important as what gets done.

Legacy isn't about what you leave behind someday.
It's about what you leave *in* people today.

The real question for leaders isn't, *"What will I be remembered for?"*

It's *"What am I shaping—daily, quietly, and consistently—through the way I lead?"*

That is the legacy that lasts. That—more than strategy, title, or tenure—is the legacy that endures.

Connect With Christina

www.leadershiplegacy.co
www.linkedin.com/in/christina-bedal-sphr-2a0a4a1
www.facebook.com/profile.php?id=61578872962383
www.instagram.com/leadershiplegacyco
@leadershiplegacyco

AVIVA'S LEGACY

By **Cristina Bernardo**
co-founder of Avocado Health

A brilliant female Latinx author by the name of Isabel Allende was once famously asked to speak about her legacy at a conference in Europe in front of thousands of listeners. She joked that *"legacy"* was truly only a *"man's word."* I can't type the exact word she used here unfortunately, though it was rather hilarious albeit slightly inappropriate for this medium. Yet what she said struck a chord with me. Was *legacy* truly a word meant only for men? And what, then, does it mean to us modern women—many of us trying to *"do it all"*?

My life of late has been, if not designed by death, perhaps built around it. The year 2020, like for so many around the world, brought immense hardship to me and my family. It brought my most beautiful third child, Aviva Lilia, into this world, and it also tragically stole her away from me on November 18, 2020, due to a rare and unknown illness. That same year also took away my beloved cousin Patrick, just 41 years old, who truly inspired me to lead a life of purpose, lost tragically to COVID. My nephew was also in a terrible car accident caused by someone who likely fell asleep behind the wheel. He survived—but lost his treasured girlfriend Jocelyn, only 31.

Death, it seemed, had found me. It awakened me to the true realities of life—the enormity of loss and the tremendous voids in between. Losing my beloved Aviva has fundamentally changed who I am at my core, shaken the life I once knew, and awakened me to all the little things I had been missing. Somehow, thankfully, I feel she has helped me find and see my own light as I never could before.

In losing Aviva, Patrick, and Jocelyn, I learned about death and what it truly means to me and to my family. Yet I also learned *how to truly live*—how to open my eyes and be present with those I love, how to believe in myself during the short time I have on this earth, and how to avoid continually doubting my worth and what I can achieve.

Losing Aviva taught me not only the depths of grief, loss, and regret but also the importance of *love, connection, and purpose*. It revealed my deep need to build a life and body of work rooted in meaning—not only for her but also for me. She showed me that what truly matters in this short life is how we show up for the people we love most, in the moments that mean the most to them and to us.

So, my legacy, you say? Perhaps it is, as Allende stated, a man's word. It wasn't something I actively thought about or pursued every day. Yet I see now that my legacy will not be in how people see me after I die, but in how I can help others to live more fully while they are still here.

I hope it will be seen that my legacy lies in helping as many parents as I can—especially women and mothers carrying the weight of so many responsibilities—*find a little peace*. To help them *discover small moments of joy*. To give them the *support they need and the community they can depend on*. To guide them toward what truly matters: those fleeting moments when *we look into the eyes of the ones we love and truly see—and are seen.*

This has led us to start Avocado Health, a 24/7 parent coach in your pocket, to provide answers, guidance, and support to parents when it matters most. I hope it can be the anchor for others that I never had through Aviva's illness and the constant support I dreamt of for my daily parenting struggles.

So perhaps, in this way, my legacy is also Aviva's.

Connect With Cristina

www.avocadohealth.ai
www.linkedin.com/in/cristinabernardokullberg
www.linkedin.com/company/avocado-health-for-all
www.instagram.com/avocado_family_health
www.instagram.com/cristinakullnardo

Write the Book That Positions You as the Authority

At She Rises Studios, we don't just publish books.
We help you launch movements, legacies, and platforms for visibility.

This is your moment to claim your place as a founder-author.

✨ Full publishing
services included

✨ You keep 100%
rights & royalties

✨ Visibility across our
media ecosystem

ENROLL NOW

OFFICIAL COLLABORATOR

EMPOWERHER CONTENT DAY 02 | 22 | 2026 ALLEGIANT STADIUM-LAS VEGAS

EMPOWERHER

POWER PARTNER PROGRAM

Join a global movement inside Allegiant Stadium and be recognized as a driving force behind one of the most powerful empowerment events in history.

APPLY TO BECOME A POWER PARTNER

EXIT OR ENTITY:

THE LEGACY CHOICE EVERY FOUNDER MAKES

By **Kelly Ann Winget**
Founder and CEO of Alternative Wealth Partners

The real question:

"How do you build a business that outlives you?" is the wrong starting point. It assumes that's the goal, and it shouldn't be the default.

Founders have to decide early: Is the legacy the exit or the entity? Both are valid. But they require completely different architectures, different sacrifices, and different definitions of success. And most founders never make the choice consciously. They drift toward one or the other based on circumstances, market pressure, or exhaustion.

If your legacy is the exit, you're building to transfer value to a buyer, to shareholders, to the next chapter you want to fund. The business was the vehicle, not the destination. There's nothing wrong with that. Some of the most impactful founders I know built something extraordinary, sold it, and deployed that capital into the next mission. The exit was the legacy.

If your legacy is the entity, you're playing a different game entirely. You're building something that carries your philosophy forward through people who didn't build it but believe in it. That's harder. It requires you to codify not just what you do, but why you do it, and then trust others to interpret that when you're no longer in the room.

And here's the part nobody wants to say out loud: even if you build for the entity, the soul still leaves with you. What remains is stewardship.

Where I actually am with Alternative Wealth Partners:

I'd be lying if I said AWP doesn't center on me right now. It does. My deal instincts, my investor relationships, my willingness to be contrarian when the market wants conformity. That's the engine. I'm not replaceable today, and I'm not pretending otherwise.

But I've made a deliberate choice: I'm building AWP as a generational business, not a liquidation event. That means every system, every investor communication, every underwriting framework has to be built like I'm not the answer. Not because I'm trying to disappear, but because the mission of democratizing generational wealth is bigger than any one person. Including me.

Do I think AWP can survive beyond me? Yes. Will it be the same? No. And I've made peace with that.

What I'm building is a philosophy and a standard that the next stewards can carry forward. Whether that's internal leadership I've developed or the next generation of my own family, they won't be running *"Kelly's company."* They'll be running a company that was shaped by how I thought, what I prioritized, and what I refused to compromise on. That's what transfers. The rest is just memory.

The Buffett truth:

Berkshire will outlive Buffett. But Buffett won't. The investor experience, the annual letters, the folksy wisdom from Omaha. That's not replicable. The stewards he's chosen will protect the portfolio and honor the principles. But the soul of Berkshire Hathaway walks out the door with him.

That's not a failure. That's just the truth about founder-led businesses. You can transfer the entity. You can transfer the assets. You can even transfer the culture if you're intentional about it. But you can't transfer you.

The founders who build generational businesses aren't the ones who figured out how to live forever through their company. They're the ones who built something worth stewarding, and then chose stewards worthy of it.

Connect With Kelly

www.alternativewealthpartners.com
www.kellyannwinget.com
www.linkedin.com/company/alternative-wealth-partners
www.linkedin.com/in/kellyannwinget
www.instagram.com/alternativewealthpartners
www.instagram.com/kellyannwinget

I WON

By **Lorien Byrne**

Five years ago, if you had asked me what success looked like, I would've said winning new freelance clients, keeping everyone happy, pushing through the exhaustion. Earning just enough to survive another month, I was freelancing day and night as a single mom, juggling deadlines, school runs, and emotional overload.

From the outside, I looked capable. *"Well done, Supermom, you're so strong. You're Winning."* On the inside, I was quietly unraveling. ADHD, anxiety, burnout, people-pleasing, and a nervous system permanently set to high alert. Surviving on caffeine, nicotine, cortisol, adrenalin and alcohol. I didn't know how to say no.

I didn't know how to rest. I didn't know how to choose myself.

My whole identity was built on surviving, not living.
And then came the loss. My life became unmanageable.

Anxiety, defensiveness, addiction, burnout… it all caught up with me at once. I was exhausted from holding up a life that didn't feel like mine anymore. I was trying to be everything for everyone. When the survival mechanisms I had been using for years stopped working. I had to surrender.

That breakdown, as painful as it was, became the doorway to everything I have today. What I didn't realize then is that sometimes the collapse isn't the rock bottom, it's the beginning of a whole new reality.

Letting go of the 'survival identity' became my biggest win. I had to rebuild slowly, gently, and honestly. My healing wasn't glamorous. It looked like therapy, AA meetings, reading about healthy boundaries, learning how my hormones and ADHD influenced my behaviour, and letting myself rest without guilt for the first time in my adult life.

Over time, I started showing up differently. Clearer. Calmer. More rooted. Breathing deeper.

And with that shift came a new definition of success.

Today, success looks like steadiness. It looks like a regulated nervous system. It looks like choosing peace over performing. Curiosity over defensiveness. It looks like working in a way that's aligned with my health, not against it. It looks like building a business that allows me to thrive instead of merely cope.

I now run my own freelance video editing company partner with global brands, and the part closest to my heart, I founded Grounded Wellness. A women's health and mindset community created from everything I learned in my own healing.

Grounded Wellness is for the woman who's been holding everything together for so long she's forgotten what she needs. It's for the woman who's overwhelmed, burnt out, hormonal, overstimulated, and tired of pretending she's fine. It's for the woman who wants to feel steady again. Things look the same from the outside, but inside she's screaming.

Through simple practices, supplements, tools, emotional education, and community, I help women reclaim calm, confidence, and clarity. I show them what I wish someone had shown me earlier: you are allowed to slow down, to regulate, to rest, to have boundaries. You are allowed to be a whole person, not just a strong one.

That is the modern win I'm committed to spreading. A success story where women don't have to break themselves to build a life they're proud of. We can say no without shame or guilt.

My biggest mission now is helping other women win too. They don't have to hustle their way to worthiness. Winning is being steady. Winning is choosing yourself. Winning is living a life you don't need to numb your way through.

And that is a victory worth building a legacy on.

Connect With Lorien

www.groundedwellness.co.za
www.instagram.com/groundedwellness_za
www.facebook.com/zagroundedwellness

© HE IS VISUAL

FAITH AND LEADERSHIP:

THE WINNING COMBINATION THAT CHANGED EVERYTHING FOR ME

By **Erin Harrigan**
Founder and Head Coach, Erin Harrigan LLC, https://erinharrigan.com

In my first business with a multi-level marketing company at the age of 42, I set out to build an empire that would free me from employee life and give my family more time. Four years into that business, with all the signs of outward success, I was reeling from emptiness, anxiety, and questioning why *"success"* didn't look or feel like I'd been promised or taught.

One Moment of Grace That Changed My Path

Feeling lost and out of answers, I contacted a business mentor and shared with her that doing all the *"right"* work and achieving the *"best"* outcomes didn't feel successful. She surprised me by saying, *"You don't know who you are or WHOSE you are. Do you have a relationship with Jesus?"*

Exhausted from my self-reliance and working from my own strength, I listened to her share about this Savior who didn't make me for hustle and grind. I decided that beautiful fall day, October 4, 2014, to surrender my life to Jesus, and that changed everything for me, my family, and my business. He eventually led me to teach other high-achieving women how to operate in business His way: fully open to His mission in the marketplace.

Merging Faith and Modern Leadership

John Maxwell says, *"Everyone deserves to be led well,"* and as a follower of Jesus, I know the only way to effectively lead is to follow His example and emulate how He worked. It's the lesson He's taught me time and time again, and it's how I help my fellow high-achieving sisters in Christ to redefine hustle and navigate success with Jesus.

Still, I am a work in progress who sometimes relies on my own strength, wisdom, and knowledge to lead. Merging faith and modern leadership is making the daily decision to practice leading from a place of humility, service, and seeking the greatest good for all those I encounter through my business. I do this by seeking His leadership first before starting every day, every task, and every conversation.

I then take action in obedience and deference to Him.

In operating this way as a leader, those I lead know they are heard, understood, and valued, which inspires them to work with excellence in partnership with me.

How can we practice compassion in business?

One definition of compassion is *"the showing of mercy or leniency towards others, especially by a leader or person of authority."*

Compassionate leaders stand on the truth and deliver it with grace, focused on the best outcome for all involved. It is compassionate to hold people to the stated expectations of a role or job, and to redirect them to work that's best suited to their gifts and talents.

Compassion is standing beside people with encouragement in good and bad times, seeing them as image bearers of God, and helping them see and realize their greatest potential.

Today, compassion is often seen as a polarizing quality and even considered a weakness for a leader. I see it as an opportunity to show someone they are cared for, valued, and a necessary part of the greater plan God has for an organization and its impact on the world.

Where faith and leadership intersect is where we truly emulate the greatest leader ever known: Jesus. When we do, our work has the opportunity to change lives and legacies. In many ways, that means we have a part in healing the world through the business we do. That's fulfilling, meaningful, and that's the kind of work I am honored to do.

Connect With Erin

www.erinharrigan.com
www.linkedin.com/in/erinharrigan
www.instagram.com/erindharrigan
www.youtube.com/@erinharrigan

POWERED BY

SHE RISES
STUDIOS

FENIX TV

02 | 22 | 2026

EMPOWERHER CONTENT DAY

ALLEGIANT STADIUM-LAS VEGAS

ONE STADIUM. 40,000 WOMEN. INFINITE IMPACT

GRAB YOUR COPY NOW

Possibility to Prosperity is an inspiring anthology featuring bold, visionary women who turned their greatest struggles into triumphs. Through honest and powerful stories, these women reveal how pain can become purpose, fear can become fuel, and setbacks can spark success. From heartbreak and burnout to rejection and failure, each chapter offers lessons in resilience, reinvention, and reclaiming one's worth. With courage and determination, these stories illuminate the path from challenge to opportunity, showing that it's never too late to rise, build, and thrive. This book reminds every reader that your struggles can be the gateway to your greatest possibilities.

amazon.com   SHE RISES STUDIOS

LEADING IN A MALE-DOMINATED WORLD

By **Doug Lawrence**
Mentoring Expert and author

Leadership is often described as gender-neutral—vision, competence, integrity, and courage should matter more than who embodies them. Yet for many women, leading in a male-dominated world is not a neutral experience. It is shaped by unspoken rules, inherited power structures, and expectations that were never designed with them in mind. To lead effectively in such environments requires not only skill, but resilience, self-awareness, and a willingness to redefine what leadership looks like.

Historically, leadership models were built around traditionally masculine traits: decisiveness, assertiveness, competition, and control. These traits are not inherently negative, but they have often been elevated at the expense of others such as collaboration, empathy, and relational intelligence.

Women stepping into leadership roles frequently find themselves navigating a double bind—expected to lead *"like men"* to be taken seriously, yet criticized when they do so for being too aggressive, cold, or unlikable. At the same time, leading with empathy and inclusivity can be dismissed as weak or insufficiently authoritative. This tension is exhausting, but it is also where meaningful change begins.

One of the first challenges women leaders face is visibility. In male-dominated spaces, women are often more noticeable and more scrutinized. Mistakes may be remembered longer, successes attributed to luck or support rather than competence. This heightened visibility can create pressure to be perfect, to over-prepare, and to work harder just to be seen as equal. Over time, this can erode confidence and contribute to burnout.

Effective leadership in this context begins with reclaiming self-trust—recognizing that competence does not require perfection and that confidence grows through experience, not constant validation.

Another significant barrier is the persistence of unconscious bias. Bias shows up in subtle ways: whose ideas are heard, who is interrupted, who is assumed to be the decision-maker. It appears in performance evaluations that reward potential in men and proven results in women, or in assumptions about availability and ambition once caregiving responsibilities are introduced. Leading in a male-dominated world requires the ability to recognize these patterns without internalizing them. The goal is not to deny bias exists, but to avoid allowing it to define one's sense of worth or capability.

Mentorship and sponsorship play a critical role in navigating these environments. Mentors provide guidance, perspective, and emotional support; sponsors actively advocate for opportunities, promotions, and visibility. Women often have access to mentors but fewer sponsors, particularly in senior leadership where power is still disproportionately held by men. Seeking out allies—regardless of gender—who are willing to use their influence is not a sign of weakness, but a strategic and necessary leadership skill. Equally important is paying that support forward by mentoring others and creating pathways for future leaders.

Leading authentically is both the greatest challenge and the greatest strength for women in male-dominated spaces. Authentic leadership does not mean ignoring the realities of the environment; it means refusing to disappear within them. It involves setting boundaries, communicating clearly, and leading from values rather than from fear of perception. Authenticity builds trust, and trust is the foundation of effective leadership. When leaders are consistent, transparent, and grounded in purpose, they create cultures where others can also show up fully.

Emotional intelligence is another powerful leadership asset, though it has often been undervalued in traditional leadership narratives. The ability to listen deeply, navigate conflict, read dynamics, and foster psychological safety is not a *"soft"* skill—it is a strategic one. In complex organizations facing constant change, leaders who can engage people, manage uncertainty, and build resilient teams are indispensable. Women leaders frequently excel in these areas, not because of gender alone, but because they have learned to lead through relationship and adaptability in environments that demand it.

It is also important to acknowledge the emotional toll of leading in spaces where one is underrepresented. Imposter syndrome, isolation, and the pressure to represent an entire group can weigh heavily. Sustainable leadership requires support systems outside the workplace—coaches, mentors, peers, and spaces where leaders can reflect honestly without performing strength. Rest, reflection, and self-compassion are not indulgences; they are leadership practices that sustain clarity and effectiveness over time.

Leading in a male-dominated world is not about becoming *"one of the guys,"* nor is it about rejecting traditionally masculine traits altogether. It is about integration—bringing the full range of leadership capacities into the room and expanding the definition of what strong leadership looks like.

When women lead with competence, courage, empathy, and authenticity, they challenge outdated norms simply by existing in their power.

Ultimately, the goal is not just individual success, but systemic change. Each woman who leads openly, mentors generously, and challenges limiting assumptions makes the path more visible for others. Over time, leadership becomes less about fitting into a mold and more about shaping a culture where diversity of thought, style, and experience is recognized as a strength. Leading in a male-dominated world is demanding, but it is also transformative—both for those who lead and for the systems they help reshape.

Connect With Doug

www.talentc.ca
www.linkedin.com/in/douglawrence-mentor
www.youtube.com/c/TalentcDougLawrence/videos
www.facebook.com/doug.lawrence.1610

SUSTAINABILITY IS FUELED BY PURPOSE & FULFILLMENT

By **Rae Ostrander**

When entrepreneurs talk about legacy, they usually obsess over what happens after they die. *Will the business survive? Will people remember my name?*

To be honest, I think that version of legacy is just ego on steroids.

As an entrepreneur and a father of two teenage daughters, I've stopped trying to control what happens when I'm gone. Instead, I focus on equipping my daughters to survive and thrive while I'm here. If they learn to effectively manage the present, their future present will also be manageable as they grow and develop.

If I transfer a business to them but they lack the skill to run it, I haven't given them a legacy; I've given them a millstone around their neck. If I transfer assets without transferring the skillset to build purpose in their lives, they'll likely just seek comfort. If that is all I do, I'm just providing them with the means to remove obstacles and avoid hard things. My legacy would be enabling atrophy rather than resourcing their growth and development.

Legacy vs. Short-Term Gain: The Lesson from Recovery

For me, this isn't just business; it's deeply personal.

Especially in difficult moments, I've experienced an overwhelming desire to escape that pain. I figured out as a teenager that alcohol is an extremely effective means of immediate short-term relief.

As you can imagine, this pattern of behavior can be very harmful, and it certainly was in my case.

Over 30 years ago, I decided to stop drinking and take responsibility for my life. Thankfully, mentors were able to convince me to begin to embrace discomfort. They encouraged me to take on challenges, and with their support, I was able to string together several small victories. The positive results introduced me to a new way to approach the challenges and obstacles of life.

Short-term relief, as appealing as it is, is how I forfeit the opportunity to have the long-term high impact outcomes that would give me a sense of deep fulfillment.

Creating a Business (and Life) That Outlives You

For a business to survive for any significant length of time, it must serve the immediate as well as long-term needs of its customers and its operational team. If the business succeeds in providing a path to deeper fulfillment that has immediate relevance to their lives, the business is "*alive*". It will continue to remain alive as long as it continues to provide this. The deeper the fulfillment it contributes to, the more that business will thrive and propel itself into the future. It's not about me; it's about being perpetually relevant to our customers and team.

My oldest daughter and I invested a tremendous amount of time and money in her pursuit of athletics. As a player who came off the bench at the highest level for her age group, she could have pursued athletic scholarships for lots of D2 or D3 universities.

I was surprised, but ultimately so proud that she decided to ratchet back her focus on athletics and chose a school and a program that align with her future goals and ambitions. She didn't let her past successes which were leading her on a great educational and vocational track, limit a change in trajectory to something that provides her with a deeper sense of purpose and fulfillment. What a difficult and courageous decision it often is to move away from the comfort and familiarity of a good situation to pursue the uncertain great one.

Defining Wealth Beyond Money

Wealth provides us with the autonomy to choose from a variety of financially viable options. Hopefully we choose the ones that provide us with the most purpose and fulfillment.

Connect With Rae

www.contrastmgmt.com
www.linkedin.com/in/rae-ostrander-784a65170

FROM SURVIVAL TO RADIANCE:

BUILDING GLO FORMATION AND BREAKING CYCLES

By **Cindy Nguyen**

I stood in front of the mirror before a client meeting, looking at my blotchy, creased makeup, and felt invisible. I was in my forties, working in medical sales in a predominantly white corporate environment where I constantly had to prove myself as a minority woman. I was rushing—again—because between work, kids, and everything else, there was never enough time. That's when I knew: something had to change.

But my journey to launching GLO Formation in May 2024 started long before that mirror moment. It started when I became a teen mom at fifteen years old.

I won't pretend it was easy. I faced judgment from family, from society, from people who saw a teenage mother and assumed they knew my story. But what they didn't see was my determination. I became the first person in my family to graduate college. I built a seventeen-year career in medical sales, navigating discrimination and fighting to be seen in rooms where I was often the only Asian face.

In 2016, I decided to pursue my dream of entering the beauty industry. But life had other plans. My father was diagnosed with stage 4 kidney carcinoma cancer, and I became his primary caregiver. For eleven months, I was at every appointment, translating medical jargon, delivering devastating news with a smile, encouraging him to keep fighting even as the data told us he was losing. When he passed in 2017, I didn't just lose my father—I lost my biggest support.

I had to put my dreams on hold again. But this time, something was different. I realized I couldn't keep pouring from an empty cup. I sought therapy, did EMDR to process childhood trauma and domestic violence I had survived but never healed from. I faced the wounds I'd been carrying since I was a little girl—wounds that had shaped how I saw myself, how I showed up in the world, how I believed I deserved to be treated.

Healing wasn't linear, but it was transformative. And in that healing, my vision for GLO Formation crystallized. This wasn't just about creating another beauty product. It was about giving women back their time and confidence.

GLO Formation's multi-use glow oil is a primer, moisturizer, and radiance booster infused with vitamins A, C, and E. It cuts your routine in half so you can show up feeling beautiful and confident—because you deserve that, no matter how busy life gets.

But GLO Formation represents something deeper for me. It's about proving that your past doesn't define your worth. That being a teen mom, a survivor of trauma, a woman who's been told to dim her light—none of that disqualifies you from building something extraordinary.

Today, I volunteer with organizations supporting survivors of human trafficking, sexual abuse, and domestic violence. These causes hold my heart because I know what it means to need someone to believe you're not damaged goods. My vision is to grow GLO Formation not just as a business, but as a platform to hire survivors and give them the second chances they deserve. Everyone deserves to know their value.

I spent years being told I couldn't compete with big brands, that I should just sell someone else's products. I pushed through the self-doubt, the paralysis, the voices that said I wasn't enough. And now, customers are buying, reordering, and sharing how GLO Formation makes them feel—confident, radiant, seen.

At forty-nine, I'm finally building the legacy I always dreamed of. Not just a beauty brand, but a movement. For every woman who's been told to shrink, to stay quiet, to dim her light—I'm here to say: You deserve to glow. Your story matters. Your dreams are valid.

This is just the beginning.

Connect With Cindy

www.gloformation.com
instagram: gloformation

SHOP NOW

GRAB YOUR COPY NOW

She Endures: Perseverance Through Pain is a heartfelt anthology honoring women who have faced life's hardest moments and chosen to rise. Through honest, powerful stories of illness, loss, heartbreak, and healing, this collection reveals how pain can shape strength and purpose. Each chapter offers hope, reminding readers that endurance is not just surviving, but growing through what we overcome. Featuring Hanna Olivas, Adriana Luna Carlos, and 11 inspiring authors, this book is a testament to the resilience of women who refuse to give up.

amazon.com   **SHE RISES** STUDIOS

GET YOUR COPY NOW

Celebrate the power of women through inspiring stories and insights.

FAITH, FREEDOM & OTHER F WORDS
RHIANNON ANDERSON

THE ABCS OF SELF-LOVE (JOURNAL)
AMIE RICH

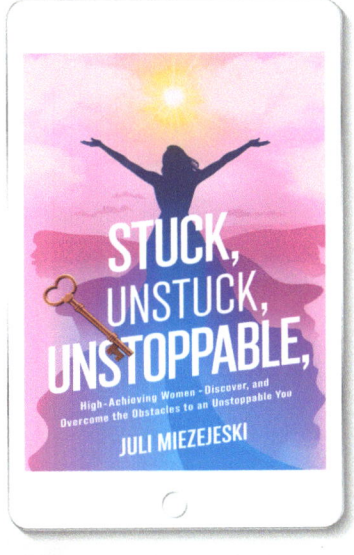

STUCK, UNSTUCK, UNSTOPPABLE
JULIA MIEZEJESKI

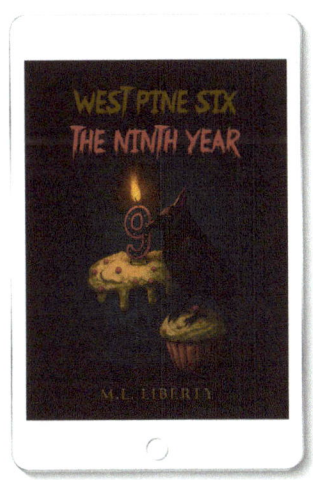

WEST PINE SIX: THE NINTH YEAR
MARIE LAURA LIBERTY

STRETCH & STRETCH JUNIOR
MICHELE KLINE

LIVING BOUNDARIES
GLEN ALEX

www.ingramcontent.com/pod-product-compliance
Lightning Source LLC
Chambersburg PA
CBHW041429120626
46547CB00002B/142